Relationships

Relationships

The Complete Black Men's Guide to Developing Healthy Relationships

You Can't Practice What You Do Not Know

Treat her like a Lady

ROBERT ALFRED TAYLOR JR.

To order additional copies of this book, contact:
Xlibris Corporation
1-888-795-4274
www.Xlibris.com
Orders@Xlibris.com
81480

Contents

ACKNOWLEDGMENTS

I would like to take the time to recognize that there is a growing problem with African American relationships. With that said, I would like to thank God for giving me the ability to see that there is a problem with African American relationships. I would also like to thank God for giving me the ability to write and try to rectify the problem.

I would like to thank President Barack Obama for challenging each and every one of us to do something that could help make America better.

To my daughter, Breanna, everything I do is for a better life for you. Daddy loves you!

To my sisters, Catina and Tania, keep striving to be the best you can be.

With love to my niece and nephew, Chris and Tania, I love you guys.

To my mother, Evaline, and dad, Robert, who brought me into this world, you encouraged me to do something positive for people; and through this book, I intend to help make a difference not only for African Americans, but also for people of all walks of life.

To my loving family, continue to pray for one another, and all things will be fine.

I could not do this without the help and support of all my friends who helped me through this. God bless you all and in everything that you do.

Hey, Jacque, thanks for all your help and putting up with all my changes.

PROLOGUE

I N TODAY'S SOCIETY, "black love" could be defined by the clothes you wear, the car you drive, the money you make, and by the job you hold. It's defined by a man's tough exterior and by the exterior beauty of a woman – the chiseled body of a young man with sagging pants or the tight, low-rise jeans worn by a fine *sista*! Black love is defined by everything except the intellect that comes with a handsome man or a gorgeous woman.

In some cases, if you have any of the above attributes, you can have that so-called man or woman of your so-called dreams! If that is all you are looking for in a relationship, then good luck with that. I say this because after the physical beauty is gone, then what do you have? Ask yourselves, is it all about the booty call? Is it all about having that eye candy on your side so that everyone can say "Damn, he or she is fine"? This guide was really written for the brothers, but the women could learn a thing or two as well. I challenge everyone reading this to get back to the basics and truly love one another for the greater good of each other, our families, and our communities.

INTRODUCTION

HAVE YOU EVER felt that you have built this image of yourself to catch the woman of your dreams, and suddenly, you're not so happy about who you've become? You want out of your current relationship because you don't feel you are being treated like you should be treated. You weren't allowed to be the man you wanted to become. Somewhere along the line, your relationship got out of hand, and you don't know what happened. You can't fix it. "Was I to blame?" you ask yourself. "Was it her fault?"

So many of us fail in our relationships these days because of a lack of relationship knowledge. We were not taught how to respect and pursue a relationship. Once in the relationship, we don't know how to properly maintain the relationship and do the things necessary to keep the negative things at bay. The main objective of entering into a relationship is to spend the rest of your life with that special someone who will help to make a loving and successful bond between two people. The objective of this guide is to help the brothers help themselves.

Let's get back to black love.

FIRST GLANCE

AT FIRST GLANCE, from a male's perspective, he is impressed by her booty! Sorry, her *beauty!* She is the most beautiful woman he has ever seen. The thoughts that are racing through his mind range from "Damn, she's fine" to "I would love to hit that." Other thoughts would be "I wonder if she will talk to me" or "I wonder how many kids she has." But at that very moment, the only thing on most guys' minds is "I really want to hit that!" Don't get me wrong, I know there are some guys who see a woman and think to themselves, "I'm going to make her my wife someday." All of these thoughts, along with others, are fine. We all are human beings and tend to have a lot of questions about the opposite sex. Let's not get totally caught up in the beauty aspect of relationships. The goal is to find out what type of person she is on the inside as well. This will help you decide if this is someone you really want to pursue. We will get to that later.

The beauty of a woman can be so overwhelming that it can intimidate a man. So much so that the fact of being embarrassed will keep him from approaching her altogether. Some would just walk away, wondering about what possibly could have been.

At first glance, a man could come up with a lot of "I wonder if she" questions. The first glance can give a false perception of what kind of person you are. Keep this in mind: once you walk out of your house, you are on display. Someone is always watching. So why not make a conscious effort to take the time to make sure you are presentable to the world, mainly to the opposite sex? That is if you are really trying to catch the attention of a potential mate. Remember, you're not the only one out there checking for someone. The way you dress says a lot about you. It could also tell others some things about you that are not true. Some guys dress tough to make other guys think they're macho. But to a woman, it could mean you're too aggressive or have a thug mentality. She will not approach you and may, through her body language, hint that she is not interested in you.

In retrospect, just be you, and dress and groom the way you want to be seen. You never know, that woman you crave and long to be with could be looking but may not like what she sees as a whole.

Don't pretend to be something you are not because, down the road, the truth will come out.

Men! Clean your fingernails, do your feet, shave, bathe, and smell good. By all means, brush your teeth and take the time to floss. If you are fortunate to have a job with benefits, get your teeth fixed! The way you look is the first thing she is going to see. So why not give her something to look at? After all, wouldn't you want that first glance to turn into a second glance and maybe a conversation?

THE APPROACH

THE APPROACH IS a little different than the first glance. This is the moment of truth. The way you look will determine if she is willing to have a conversation with you. The way you present yourself will determine if she is going to stay around and chat with you. There are all kinds of women who have very different taste in men. If you approach a woman and she rejects you, it may be that you are not her type, not that you are a bad person or ugly. However, just keeping it real, you could be ugly to her. It could also be that she judged you too soon and did not give herself a chance to meet a really good guy.

Remember, looks are not everything, but they play a major part in today's society. Men and women have this thing with "I want a certain kind of person" in their minds. They have a mental picture of what that person is going to look like. That's what they seek when they are out and about. Sometimes, this works, and you find the person of your dreams. More times than not, you may find the looks but not the intellect that was supposed to come with the looks! Damn!

Getting back to the approach, oftentimes this can be one of the hardest parts of the whole boy-meets-girl or man-meets-woman process. For instance, she may be popular among her peers, and you think she would never give you the time of day. You may feel that financially you are not up to par, and she is out of your league. She could be drop-dead gorgeous, and you get intimidated by her beauty. Yes, I said intimidated by her beauty! Don't act like that doesn't happen. I see and hear it all the time. Have you or one of your buddies ever made the comment "Man she is fine"? You think, "Will she talk to me?" Intimidated by the beauty! Sometimes, it just comes down to you really not knowing what to say to her, but you know that you have to say something to her. This is common, along with a host of other things that will keep a man from approaching a woman.

Fellas, you have to know and remember a few key things when you're getting ready to interact with a woman. First, you have to know she is human. No matter how attractive she is, she does have her flaws as well. She may be thinking the same way you are, and she is just waiting for you to approach her. Some women believe that it is the man's job to make the first move. And remember, *no* is just a word! Don't let this word keep you from approaching the opposite sex. The word *no* is just the opening of another door for someone else to come into your life to make you happy. Don't get upset and tuck your tail or resort to trying to belittle her because your ego may have been a little bruised. She may let you know that you are not the one for her, but she may know someone who she thinks may be a better fit for you. So don't be so quick to give the cold shoulder. Getting turned down is nothing, and let's face it, we all have been turned down before. And we all lived to tell about it. You ever hear the saying "It's not for everyone"? Well, everyone you approach will not be the one for you. So keep it moving!

Once you approach the girl of your dreams, try not to be so aggressive. A woman likes a man to be a man, but she likes to see a little gentleness and finesse as well. I suggest easing into the conversation. On the first approach, you don't know her likes and dislikes. So while engaging in conversation, it's always good to try and find a common ground to talk about. Laughter is one of the oldest guaranteed icebreakers known to man. All women love a man who can make her laugh and smile. Making a woman laugh without acting like a clown helps ease the tension and calms the nerves for both parties involved. It's okay to compliment her, but be respectful. Nowadays, men don't compliment women as much. Some women don't know how to take a compliment either.

Women are beautiful; and they come in all shapes, sizes, and colors. She has more than just a nice backside or a great set of breasts. Take the time to listen to her speak. Listen to the tone of her voice. Look at her beautiful set of pearly whites (teeth). Take the time to look her in the eyes. Check out her voluptuous, well-made-up lips and hold on to her every word. Notice the care of her fingernails and hands. Compliment her hair or her style altogether. Eye contact is very important because a woman wants to know that you're into her only and not into every other woman who walks by as well.

Your body language is equally important. Even though you may be a little nervous, try to remain calm and confident in your approach. Speak and respond with intelligence and clarity. Even though you're speaking to the most beautiful woman you've ever laid eyes on, it's imperative to remain calm and maintain your composure. Remember to be who you are, and everything will work out fine. You never know, that conversation could last for hours!

THE INTRODUCTION

IN ALL RELATIONSHIPS, honesty is best. The introduction must be respectful and kind but not weak. It should not be full of game. Don't give out all your information during the introduction. As time goes by, and if you're fortunate enough to see her again, a little more information will be relinquished. You don't want to give out all your information to someone you may not ever talk to again.

The introduction does not require touching. Extending your hand for a handshake will do just fine. A gentle touch on the shoulder to get her attention is okay, but make sure she knows you don't mean any disrespect by the touch. If during the introduction the woman asks you what is it you want from her, be honest, and let her know that you admire her beauty and you are interested in getting to know what type of person she is. You don't want to end up with a beautiful monster.

There is a saying going around that goes "It's not tricking if you got it." This means if you have money, you should spend it with reckless abandon on the girl of your choosing. This is usually done so that you can get the girl and maybe get her to do whatever it is you want her to do. You don't have to spend a lot of money on a real woman. Just do what is necessary at the moment. If you start off spending tons of money in the beginning, she is going to expect that throughout the relationship. It can cause a problem down the road if you cannot maintain this type of behavior.

Realize that from this moment on, you are laying the foundation of the relationship. You want the foundation of the relationship to be strong and steady, not built with bad concrete. This means being honest. Notice how many times honesty comes up in this guide. It's really that important in any relationship. So get her to know you and not your wallet. She will get there soon enough! A woman doesn't want to feel like she is being purchased. Also, keep in mind that some guys spend on women because their conversation isn't really that strong. They use spending as a means of doing something positive to get the attention of the woman. Now don't get me wrong, there are some women out there who will let you buy them. We are not talking about them.

Nowadays, women have their own money, so many of them will not be impressed with yours. Once the doors of conversation open and you all start talking about what you do for a living, be honest and say what it is that you do. Don't make up titles to make the job sound better than it is. Most women just want to know that you have a job and a paycheck coming in. You have to give the woman honest answers so that she can make an honest decision to herself if she wants to pursue a possible relationship with you based on the information you are giving her. She should be doing the same as well. Honesty goes both ways! Paint a realistic picture of who you are and not a picture of who you would like to be.

It's okay to share your dreams and ambitions for the future. That shows that you have goals, and hopefully, you are working hard to attain those goals. Women love men with positive goals and oftentimes get involved with the guy so they can be a part of the transformation of positive growth. Remember, the proof is always in what you do, not what you say!

Know this: the introduction is not just for you. You have given her an open invitation to come in and be a part of your world as well. So make sure your world is calm and not full of unwanted baggage. For example, baby momma drama, tons of children by different women, etc. These things will keep you from having a promising future with the woman of your dreams.

Maintain your swagger during the introduction. Now some men get swagger mixed up with arrogance and an overbearing "It's all about me" attitude. Sorry, that's not it, bro! *Swagger* is the confidence in the way you approach, the overall smooth presence that says to a woman, "Why not me?" But not so smooth that she thinks you're a con. If you are in the club or restaurant, offer to buy her a drink to break the ice. This is not trickery! Discuss the fruit at the grocery store without comparing the fruit to her body parts. Discuss books at the bookstore. Whatever it is that is worth discussing at the time. This helps to establish common interest at the time.

CONTACT INFORMATION

O NCE YOU'RE SURE she's into you and the conversation is going in a positive direction, it's okay to proceed with asking for her phone number. I've heard conversations from men saying, "Don't call her right away. Give it three days before you call." Who made up this rule? The bad part about this is that I used to follow this rule. The whole idea of getting the phone number is to get in contact with someone you can't wait to talk to again. Now again, be respectful of her time. She may work certain hours, be a part of some type of organization, or have a time set aside to workout, among other things. Get to know these things about her and you will be knowledgeable of her schedule, and she will let you know what the good times to call are. Just be considerate of the times you call. If she is interested in you, she is going to make it a point to include you in her schedule. Discuss texting before you start doing so. Don't be that guy who calls every minute of the day. This sends a red flag to her. It makes her wonder, "Isn't he supposed to be at work or doing something positive?" Don't become a stalker.

Exchanging addresses is also an invitation for you to enter into her very private space and vice versa. Don't be so anxious to invite someone over to your home. That opens the door to people just popping up at unexpected times. Don't you become the person who keeps popping up! This goes for the ladies as well. When going out on your first several dates, it is okay to meet at a place that you both agreed on. Just think, if it doesn't work out, they still have access to your home. Basically, take your time when it comes to giving out your information. As time goes by and you spend more time with each other, you will begin to share personal information.

FIRST DATE

THE FIRST DATE has arrived! This is what you have been waiting for. Up to this part, you have done everything right. You've seen someone you were physically attracted to, you've used the right approach, your introduction was to the point and respectful, the conversation you had with her was great, and you got the digits! She has now accepted the offer to go out on a date with you. This can be the beginning of a wonderful relationship if you play your cards right. Now she is really going to check you out. This is where she is going to see if you have any good upbringing.

So you're getting ready for your date, and you all have decided where you are going. Dress appropriately! If you're going out to eat, dress in some nice dinner attire. If you're going bowling, dress in clothes that will allow you to move. If you're an older guy, dress your age! If you're a younger guy, dress like you have some sense! Again, a woman likes to see a well-put-together brother! That means you have to come correct. Shower, shave, and get your hair cut. When applying your cologne, do *not* put so much on that it is too unbearable to be around. Brush your teeth, floss, and rinse with mouthwash. My mom used to tell me all the time to make sure I was wearing good underwear because you never know if you're going to get into an accident. Wear the right watch and accessories, but don't break out the Mr. T starter kit. Make sure your nails are clipped and cleaned. Clean your ears inside and out. Make sure the whip (car) is clean inside and out and smells good and pleasant.

Since it is your first date, you may want to stop by the florist to pick up some nice flowers. I don't know a woman who doesn't like flowers. Once you arrive to pick her up, make sure you open the door for her. Keep your eyes open as well. Once she is in the car, check to see if she reaches over to unlock your door. The old-school mothers and fathers told me this is an act of unselfishness. It means she cares about you as well! Now if you guys decide to meet up somewhere, it would be really cool to make the necessary arrangements. A nice flower would still be nice for the table.

Presentation is everything!

Once she arrives, compliment her appearance. A gentle hug is necessary – it gives you a chance to take in her aroma, and it gives her a chance to take in your scent as well. Using all the senses is great when interacting with the opposite sex. Keep it real. Don't order food you don't know about unless you both decide it is something you all want to experience together for the first time. This makes for pleasant memories later on down the line. Be spontaneous when dating. Dating doesn't only require eating, drinking, and going to the movies. Even though we know these things are fun, there are other things to do as well, such as going to the museum, walking hand in hand while window-shopping, having a nice spring picnic for two in the park, horseback riding, chilling on the beach at sunset, going on a hiking trip, and following it up with dinner. I could go on, but you get the message. Step out of the box sometimes.

When out on your first date, don't look to have sex on the first date! That is not your agenda. Your agenda is to get to know this person with no strings attached and let them get to know you as well so that this relationship grows. Now don't get me wrong, I can't tell two grown people when to have sex. I'm just saying not to make it the only interest in the relationship. After the sex is gone, all you have is each other. So hopefully through the years, you all have established other things that keep your attention on your mate.

Back to the date. After the night is over and the date was a great success, you have a couple of things you can do. If you guys had a great time and really don't want the date to end just yet, how about a nice place to have a drink, some fine music, and a ton of laughs? If the date is over, gently kiss her on the cheek and tell her what a great time you had and that you would like to see her again. Walk her to her car to make sure she gets into her car safely. Have her call you when she gets home to make sure she made it in okay. This could lead to more conversation as well. If you picked her up, drive her home and take the time to tell her what a great time you had and you would like to see her again. Remember to open the door for her at all times. Some women are not used to a man opening the doors for them, so you might have to let her know by saying, "I'll get the door for you." At any rate, continue to be a gentleman throughout the date.

If she invites you in after the date, that does not mean you are going to get some. So don't put pressure on her to do so. She may just really enjoy your company. Her inviting you in is a form of trust she has for you! Most times, getting invited in can lead to other things. Make sure you are paying attention to what is going on and make good decisions. It's hard, I know, but sometimes, we have to make the right decision, and sometimes, that decision is not to let the little head make the decision for you. The flesh is weak! Man, I know!!!

If the date did not go well, it's okay. Accept the fact that the relationship is not going any further from here. Remain respectful, and you may have just made yourself another friend instead of a mate. Friendship is always good, and besides, as friends, you sometimes find out that you have a lot of things in common, and over time, it could evolve into a relationship.

COURTING

COURTING! THIS IS the phase where you show and prove. This is the time to do all those things you said you liked to do and all those experiences you said you would like to share with her is here. Check this out: when you are courting a woman, you are not just trying to impress her. There are other people who will start to come into the picture. Friends, family, haters of happiness, and children are people who will be coming around, trying to find out who she is spending all this time with. These people are wondering why their time has been cut in half. Now don't get me wrong, you're not in this to make a great impression on them. But it helps to have the other people who love her and care about her well-being like you as well.

In today's society, the courting phase is not being practiced like it should be. Women make it easier for men to come into their lives and, in the end, find out later that they are really not compatible at all. The sex in the relationship comes into play too fast. There are a lot of regrets for even having the relationship. It just all went to hell, and a lot of time has been wasted. Now the good thing about this is that if you are smart, you know not to pursue a relationship the wrong way again. But if you don't really know how to pursue a relationship correctly, you end up making the same mistakes over and over again. Not good!

Men! All women love to be spoiled! All women love flowers and candy and want to live the dream of having their knight in shining armor. Women want to live happily ever after with the man of their dreams, and that could be *you*!

You have made a conscious decision to pursue this woman. Now let's get busy. Courting is basically a trial period – a proving session, if you will. Remain respectful at all times. Be creative when you are buying her things that show her you care. If you guys are walking by a store with small trinkets in the window and she happens to mention she really likes it, go back later and purchase it for her and surprise her with it later. Great brownie points!

All women love to receive flowers, especially at her place of employment. It shows the other women at the job that she has someone on the outside that is thinking about her and, in turn, impresses her as well. Now a lot of women these days are so busy they don't have time to cook. So if you get a chance to cook her a really good meal, I'm sure she will love you for that. If you do not know how to cook, that's okay too! Buy a meal from her favorite restaurant and bring it home and set it up as if it was a home-cooked meal. Explain to her that you are not the best cook around but you wanted to do something special for her.

Courting does not always mean buying her something. It means opening the door for her, making her smile at every meeting the two of you have. If you guys attend church on Sundays, invite her to your church. Make a date to go to her church as well. This also shows the family that you care enough for her to worship with her.

Now, I repeat, do not do things that you really don't like to do. That's fake, and we are not getting into this type of behavior. Honesty is always the best policy. I know you've heard that before.

When you meet the family for the first time, just be yourself. This is your chance to see what type of family she comes from. If the family acts like a bunch of hooligans, then there is a slight chance she may be putting up a front for you. The apple doesn't fall too far from the tree. There are some families that act crazy, but there is someone in the family who has good sense. Hope and pray that you found that one. But really take the time to get to know the family, especially her mom and dad. Don't plan on being phony with Dad because he is not having a bunch of foolishness for his baby girl. But you're an upstanding man anyway, so we don't have to worry about that. Her mother is checking you out as well. If you impress Mom, you're halfway in the door. It's okay to bring Mom flowers and a bottle of wine for the household! Never show up empty-handed in someone's home. Bringing a gift to someone's home is a way of saying thank you for allowing you to spend time in their home.

A woman also likes to see how you interact with your mom and sisters as well. This shows your lady friend a little bit of how you are going to treat her. If you treat your mom disrespectfully, then there is a chance that you will treat her with disrespect down the line. It is a privilege to introduce a woman to your mom. Everyone doesn't get to meet Mom. This shows the woman that she is special and you cared enough to take her around your family.

While courting your lady friend, it's always a good idea to be spontaneous and fun. Do things you wouldn't normally do, like going for walks in the park or by the lake. Exercising together is always a great idea. You all can motivate each other to keep going. Go out for ice cream. Do things you have always wanted to do but never wanted to do alone.

Now hear this, men! The things you do to catch the woman is the things you need to continue to do throughout your relationship. This is why I say, be honest with her, and do things you like to do and things you both like to do together. That way, it is not like pulling teeth! If the courting phase is spicy, fun, and enjoyable, there is no reason why the relationship shouldn't remain this way as well! Never get so relaxed that you forget what got you to this point in the first place. Girls just want to have fun! I find this to be true. I also find that if it is you that she is having fun with, it is you she will stay with. You feel me? Happy courting!

MARRIAGE OR INTIMACY FIRST

Marriage or intimacy first is a scary thought, right? Wrong! Why is it wrong, you ask? Simple! You put in all that work to get to this point. You all have arrived to a point where you have to make a very important decision in your relationship. That is, if you are a couple who are trying to do things the right way in order to preserve the wholeness of the relationship. Yes, you all have been out a number of times and enjoy each other's company to the max. You always want to be around each other because it makes you feel good to be able to relax and have conversation that is stimulating! The perfect couple doing the right thing! But what's next? All the time you think of her, and you want to take it to the next level, but you want to respect her. As a woman, she doesn't want to look as though she is easy and wants to keep you around for the long haul. See, the things that go through a woman's mind is "If I give it up to him, will he stay around? I don't want to make him wait forever, I may lose this guy. I don't want to have sex with him, but if I don't, will he go searching somewhere else?" Women also want to know if you can please her as well.

Men! Your job is to be open in your communication with her, and she should be honest and open with you as well. We all know the right way is to get married and then have sex! Correct? Sure it is, but in today's society, this way of doing things is not being practiced. Sex as a whole is not held sacred anymore. Everyone is having sex, and no one seems to be getting satisfied! Why is that, you ask? Well, I will tell you. In a relationship, there are three ties that bind the relationship: the man, the woman, and God! In most relationships, people go into it the wrong way. Their main purpose is to get the opposite sex in the sack! You have men saying to each other, "Why buy the cow when you can get the milk for free?" You don't have to test the sex to determine whether or not she is the one for you. If she has everything else that is needed to have a great relationship, then the sex will be great. If the sex is not great, with the right conversation expressing what it is that everyone wants out of their sexual experience, it tends to make for a very great sex life for the both of you. I say this because you can grow as a team in all facets of the relationship. As husband and wife, you can explore each other sexually and not feel guilty about the pleasure you're feeling because it is your significant other. Wouldn't you want a woman who knows your body and knows how to please you just the way you like it? Wouldn't you want to be able to please your woman the way she wants to be pleased as well? You don't have to go through several different women to get that one thing she can do best and off to the other to receive whatever it is that she has to offer, and so on and so on. Trying to take care of several women is draining. It may seem cool when you're young and dumb, but it gets old. And who needs all that extra drama?

Sex is so much better when you can share it with someone you are mentally connected with, emotionally connected with, and above all else, spiritually connected with. It doesn't mean so much when the only connection you have with someone is those couple of drinks and great sexual experiences you shared. Let's get to that grown-up level and stop searching for false love.

The main reason for being in a partnership is to grow old with the one you love, not growing old and deciding that she doesn't look as young and as beautiful as she used to. Don't ship her out because what you are getting rid of are wisdom, love, honesty, friendship, support, trust, history, and family. She may not look as young as she used to, but neither do you! The happier you are with your mate, the better you look as you get older! Don't be so eager to replace the one you're with with a younger version. The mentality of the younger model is not as seasoned as the one you were with, and you end up starting all over again. Besides, at this point, you're no spring chicken either! Here's the kicker! Once the sex is gone, what are you left with? Well, I will tell you that as well. If you grow old with the person you worked so hard to get, you have chemistry and understanding of each other. You have gotten to a point in life where just the sight of the other is great! You can talk about anything and nothing, and it is still the best conversation you ever had! With the replacement, you may not have anything in common. You find yourself comparing the new one with the old one and finding out in your twisted mind that the one you had was the best one for you. Why? Because she knew you better than you knew yourself! In this new relationship, you spend all your time trying to keep up with this young version and understanding what this person is all about. Oh yeah, you are older, so some of that time may be spent wondering if she has a younger version of you on the side. Isn't life *great?*

Men! Make love to her mind first, and the body will follow! Don't act like a pimp and try to manipulate her mind by telling her she is nothing without you just so you can run the show. Love hard on your woman! Cherish your woman! Protect your woman! Listen to your woman! Encourage your woman! *Satisfy* your woman! This makes for a happy man! I have to keep it real and know that everyone will not follow the guide that I have written for you. I have to tell you if you are going to pursue relationships the wrong way, be as safe as possible. Protect yourself and the woman as well. Take the time to think about why it is that your relationships keep failing. A real man is not afraid to ask questions. A real man does not mind listening.

I hope I said something here to make a difference in the lives of those who are trying to live better lives. The goal is to bring people together the right way to live happy and long lives together. I figure that if I can bring people together and they live longer lives together, then we can bring back the two household families. Maybe we can bring back the older grandmother and grandfather. Bring back the respect that our young women deserve.

Women! Allow yourself to be respected. I said this because I know you all are reading this guide as well. We men are doing what we have to do to make relationships work, and we need you to do the same thing. If we all respect each other, we can all learn and grow for the betterment of our relationships as a whole.

THE EVER-CHANGING PHYSICAL APPEARANCE

OUR BODIES ARE changing every day, and it is our job to make sure we are being the best that we can be. Back in the days, we were athletic-looking in our appearance, and the ladies had the Coca-Cola bottle shape. Those were the days, weren't they? As the years roll along, our eating habits change, babies are born, and the fellas spend a lot more time drinking beer and watching the games on Sunday. Then there are the pressures of work as well as taking care of Mom and Dad. The time spent in the gym has been cut down and, to some, have been cut out altogether.

I bring this about because men tend to put a lot pressure on their women when it comes to their physical appearance. For some odd reason, men want their women to maintain that young, physical beauty that they once had some many years ago. And then the women begin to stress out because they think they are not as beautiful to their spouses. Then the crazy diets, the plastic surgeries, liposuctions, more makeup, and all the other things that really make some look generic and not so attractive come into play. The thing we men must remember is that we cannot ask a woman to do things that we are not willing to do ourselves. We have to encourage our women to take care of themselves, and they have to do the same as well. This takes unwanted stress out of the relationship. Take walks together, watch what you eat as a family, and love each other more than ever. Make sure you are getting your regular checkups and join a gym together. The whole purpose of the relationship is to take care of each other, not to criticize each other. If you want her to lose the baby fat, you could stand to lose the beer belly!

To the ladies who are reading this, you can't use the excuse of "It's baby weight" when the baby is fifteen years old and in high school.

There is this thing called *genes* that have something to do with the way we look as we get older. Some believe that if you want to know what your woman is going to look like at an older age, look at her mother. For the most part, this is true. If the mother has lived a fast and not-so-good life, she may look a little worn down. If the daughter is living a somewhat good life, she could look a little better than Mom, and vice versa.

Bottom line is we need to take care of one another and not criticize the physical appearance of our significant others. Let's encourage and care for one another, and we can grow old and laugh and be happy with one another for the rest of our lives.

THINGS TO REMEMBER

1. Just because she fits the physical description of what you would like doesn't mean she has the intellect that you would like to come with it.

2. Money doesn't determine the type of guy you are. It just shows your financial status.

3. Look for women who have things in common with you.

4. If you feel she is worth pursuing, don't give up on the first sign of rejection.

5. Do new and exciting things.

6. Get to know each other's likes and dislikes.

7. Listen to what is being said at all times.

8. Be respectful!

9. It can be tricking if you got it!

10. Be approachable.

11. Be encouraging, not insulting.

TWELVE THINGS NEEDED TO HAVE A SUCCESSFUL RELATIONSHIP

God

Chivalry

Respect

Honesty

Love

Romance

Trust

Friendship

Loyalty

Discipline

Intimacy

Obedience

A LITTLE SOMETHING FOR THE WOMEN

HEY LADIES, I know you thought I forgot about you. I didn't forget you at all. Let me start by saying that women have the power! Everything that we do is to get the attention of a woman. It starts at a young age. When we were young, we started by hanging out with the coolest crew in school. We would dress cool so you all could take notice. We love to play sports for ourselves, but the bonus was getting the attention of the most popular and prettiest girls in the school.

Some guys skipped college and hit the streets so they could maintain the fresh dress code and drive the most expensive cars with rims. They were trying to attract them around the way girls. Some brothers went to college and chased that degree to get that good job so they can bring in that legal cash so that they can get the girl of their dreams.

The men know how to step to you and make everything they say sound so promising and true. They do this to land the girls of their interest. This type of approach works more so now than ever. Back in the day, men had to talk and impress a little more to land the young lady.

Nowadays, the women give it up too easy! The girls are becoming mothers too soon, and the women find themselves going through a lot of meaningless relationships. You guys have to start holding these guys accountable. Don't be so quick to give up your love nest. You are more deserving of just one-night stands. Don't always go for the fortune and the fame. The fast life also has a fast aging process. There are a lot of reasons why men approach women the wrong way. There are a lot of reasons why women allow negative things in their lives as well.

That is another book.

Be careful out there, and by all means, demand your respect and look for more than just a handsome face and nice body. Look for more meaningful things from a man.

PRECIOUS

YOU GREW UP feeling all alone with no one to turn to. You felt that the only way to feel love was to have a baby – someone that you can love and someone who will love you back. You grew up with all these fantasies of meeting the man of your dreams and having children and living happily ever after. High school and college were supposed to be the best years of your life. Somewhere along the lines, things got confusing, and everything started to get complicated. As time went by, you started to meet men who treated you badly. They told you how fine you were and complimented you until they got what they came for – sex! You let the guys have sex with you because it made you feel wanted at the time. After the sex was gone, so was the feeling of being wanted. You never had a real man tell you how beautiful you are and really mean it. Never have you been around a man who really respected you as a person. You were never encouraged to have your own things. You were dependent upon men to make ends meet and pay your bills in exchange for sex. The times have changed, and you have had enough. You wanted to make things better for yourself. You went to school to get the education you left behind. You changed your appearance to be more respected but still sexy and adored. Other things came into play, like he is a down-low brother. This guy is fine, but he is gay. There seems to be a shortage of men. But you kept pushing on to be the best person you could become. Still, I think you're special! I think you are the mother of this earth. You are the definition of strength, structure, and struggle! You are the flower that stands strong in the concrete jungle! You are the push when we need it. You are the voice of reason when we need it most. You are that breath of fresh air that we men long to have. That smile on your face can't be replaced. I love the sway in your waist.

When I look into your eyes, I see the look of love. When I hear your voice, it's like a sweet song I want to hear all the time. Damn, you're fine! I know times get hard, but remember, you are the reason we are the way we are. Love is never easy! Be strong, and you will survive. And still, to me, you're *precious*.